Christmas Carols

ILLUSTRATED by MARIAN CLARK

CHRONICLE BOOKS
SAN FRANCISCO

First published in 1994 by
The Appletree Press Ltd
19–21 Alfred Street, Belfast BT2 8DL
Tel. +44 (0) 1232 243074
Fax +44 (0) 1232 246756
Copyright © The Appletree Press Ltd. 1994

A Little Book of Christmas Carols

First published in the United States in 1995 by
Chronicle Books, 275 Fifth Street,
San Francisco, CA 94103

ISBN: 0-8118-0937-4

9 8 7 6 5 4 3 2 1

Contents

Angels We Have Heard On High 50

Away in a Manger 22

Coventry Carol, The 6

Deck the Hall 4

Ding! Dong! Merrily on High 18

First Nowell, The 31

God Rest You Merry, Gentlemen 28

Good King Wenceslas 34

Hark! The Herald Angels Sing 16

Holly and the Ivy, The 40

I Saw Three Ships Come Sailing In 20

In the Bleak Mid-Winter 8

It Came Upon the Midnight Clear 26

Joy to the World 52

O Christmas Tree 56

O Come All Ye Faithful 12

O Little Town of Bethlehem 24

Once, in Royal David's City 44

Rocking 38

See, Amid the Winter's Snow 48

Silent Night! Holy Night! 14

Three Kings of Orient 46

Twelve Days of Christmas, The 58

Wassail, Wassail, all over the Town 42

We Wish You a Merry Christmas 36

What Child is This 54

While Shepherds Watched their Flocks by Night 10

Deck the Hall

E   F#m   E

Deck the hall with boughs of — hol - ly, Fa la la la la, la

B   E

la la la. 'Tis the sea - son to be — jol - ly,

F#m   E   F#m7 E   B

Fa la la la la, la la la la. Don we now our

E   B   F#   B

gay ap - pa - rel, Fa la, — la la, la la la,

Troll the an - cient Yule - tide ca - rol,

Fa la la la la, la la la la.

See the blazing Yule before us,
Fa la la la la, la la la la.
Strike the harp and join the chorus,
Fa la la la la, la la la la.
Follow me in merry measure,
Fa la, la la, la la la,
While I tell of Yule-tide treasure,
Fa la la la la, la la la la.

Fast away the old year passes,
Fa la la la la, la la la la.
Hail the new, ye lads and lasses,
Fa la la la la, la la la,
Sing we joyous all together,
Fa la, la la, la la la,
Heedless of the wind and weather,
Fa la la la la, la la la la.

The Coventry Carol

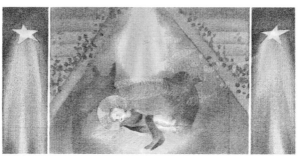

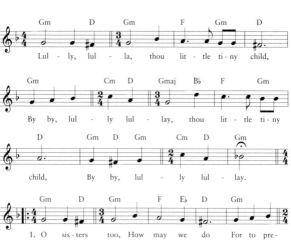

Lul - ly, lul - la, thou lit - tle ti - ny child,

By by, lul - ly lul - lay, thou lit - tle ti - ny

child, By by, lul - ly lul - lay.

1. O sis - ters too, How may we do For to pre-

Herod, the king,
In his raging,
Charged he hath this day
His men of might,
In his own sight,
All young children to slay.

That woe is me,
Poor child for thee!
And ever morn and day,
For thy parting
Neither say nor sing
By by, lully lullay!

In the Bleak Mid-Winter

In the bleak mid - win - ter Frost - y wind made moan. Earth stood hard as ir - on, Wa - ter like a stone: Snow had fall - en, snow on snow, Snow__ on __ snow,

In the bleak mid - win - ter,   Long _ a - go.

Our God, heaven cannot hold him
Nor earth sustain:
Heaven and earth shall flee away
When he comes to reign:
In the bleak mid-winter
A stable place sufficed
The lord God almighty
Jesus Christ.

Angels and archangels
May have gathered there,
Cherubim and seraphim
Thronged the air:
But only his mother
In her maiden bliss
Worshipped the beloved
With a kiss.

What can I give him.
Poor as I am?
If I were a shepherd
I would bring a lamb;
If I were a wise man,
I would do my part;
Yet what I can I give him
Give my heart.

While Shepherds Watched their Flocks by Night

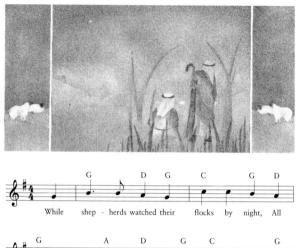

While shep - herds watched their flocks by night, All seat - ed on the ground, The an - gel of the Lord came down, And glo - ry shone a - round.

"Fear not," said he (for mighty dread
Had seized their troubled mind),
"Glad tidings of great joy I bring
To you and all mankind.

"To you in David's town this day
Is born of David's line
The Saviour, who is Christ the Lord;
And this shall be the sign:

"The Heavenly Babe you there shall find
To human view displayed,
All meanly wrapped in swathing bands,
And in a manger laid."

Thus spake the seraph; and forthwith
Appeared a shining throng
Of angels, praising God, who thus
Addressed their joyful song;

"All glory be to God on high,
And to the earth be peace;
Good will henceforth from heaven to men
Begin and never cease."

O Come all ye Faithful

O come all ye faith-ful, Joy-ful and tri - um-phant, O come ye, O come ye to Beth - le - hem! Come and be - hold him, Born the King of An - gels! O come, let us a - dore him! O come, let us a - dore him! O

come, let us a-dore___ him, Christ___ the Lord!

God of God,
Light of Light,
Lo! he abhors not the Virgin's womb;
Very God,
Begotten, not created. *Chorus*

See how the shepherds
Summoned to his cradle,
Leaving their flocks, draw nigh to gaze!
We, too will thither
Bend our heart's oblations. *Chorus*

Let star-led chieftains,
Magi, Christ adoring,
Offer him incense, gold and myrrh;
We to the Christ-child
Bring our hearts' oblations. *Chorus*

Child, for us sinners,
Poor and in the manger,
Faith we embrace thee with love and awe;
Who would not love thee,
Loving us so dearly? *Chorus*

Sing, choirs of angels
Sing in exultation!
Sing, all ye faithful to heaven above:
'Glory to God
In the highest'. *Chorus*

Yea, Lord, we greet thee,
Born this happy morning;
Jesu, to thee be glory given,
Word of the Father
Now in flesh appearing. *Chorus*

Silent Night! Holy Night!

Si - lent night! ho - ly night! Sleeps the earth, calm and quiet; Love - ly Child, now take thy rest: On thy mo - ther's gen - tle breast Sleep in hea - ven - ly peace! Sleep in hea - ven - ly peace!

Silent night! holy night!
When thou smil'st, love-beams bright
Pierce the darkness all around;
Son of God, thy birth doth sound
Our salvation's hour!
Our salvation's hour!

Silent night! holy night!
From the heaven's golden height
Christ descends, the earth to free;
Grace divine! by thee we see
God in human form!
God in human form!

Silent night! holy night!
God above at that sight
Doth with fatherly love rejoice,
While earth's peoples, with one voice,
Jesus their brother proclaim!
Jesus their brother proclaim!

Hark! The Herald Angels Sing

Hark! the he - rald an - gels sing:___
'Glo - ry to the new - born King! Peace on earth and
mer - cy mild, __ God and sin - ners re - con - ciled!'
Joy - ful, all ye na - tions rise! __ Join the tri - umph

of the skies! U‑ni‑ver‑sal Na‑ture say: 'Christ the Lord is born to‑day!' Hark! the he‑rald an‑gels sing: 'Glo‑ry__ to the new‑born King!'

Christ, by highest heaven adored,
Christ the everlasting Lord;
Late in time behold him come,
Offspring of a Virgin's womb.
Veiled in flesh the Godhead see!
Hail the incarnate Deity,
Pleased as man with man to dwell:
Jesus, our Emmanuel!

Chorus

Hail the heaven‑born Prince of peace!
Hail the Sun of Righteousness!
Light and life to all he brings,
Risen with healing in his wings.
Mild, he lays his glory by,
Born that man no more may die,
Born to raise the sons of earth,
Born to give them second birth.

Chorus

Ding! Dong! Merrily on High

Ding! dong! mer- ri -ly on high In heav'n the bells are ring - ing; Ding! dong! ve- ri -ly the sky Is riv'n with an - gels sing - ing. Glo - - - - -

- ri - a! Ho - san - na in ex - cel - sis!

E'en so here below, below,
Let steeple bells be swungen,
And 'Io, io, io!'
By priest and people sungen.

Chorus

Pray you, dutifully prime
Your matin chime, ye ringers!
May you beautifully rime
Your evetime song, ye singers!

Chorus

I Saw Three Ships Come Sailing In

I saw three ships come sail - ing in, On
Christ - mas Day, on Christ - mas Day, I
saw three ships come sail - ing in, On
Christ - mas Day in the morn - ing.

(Verse style: I saw three ships come sailing in,
        On Christmas Day, on Christmas Day,
       I saw three ships come sailing in,
        On Christmas Day in the morning).

And what was in those ships all three?

Our Saviour Christ and his lady.

Pray, whither sailed those ships all three?

O, they sailed into Bethlehem.

And all the bells on earth shall ring,

And all the angels in heaven shall sing,

And all the souls on earth shall sing.

Then let us all rejoice again!

Away in a Manger

A - way in a＿ man - ger, no＿ crib for a
bed, The＿ lit - tle Lord Je - sus laid＿
down his sweet head; The stars in the＿
bright sky looked down where he lay The＿

lit – tle Lord Je - sus a – sleep on the hay.

The cattle are lowing,
the Baby awakes,
But little Lord Jesus,
no crying he makes.
I love thee,
Lord Jesus!
Look down from the sky,
And stay by my cradle till morning is nigh.

Be near me,
Lord Jesus:
I ask thee to stay
Close by me forever,
and love me, I pray;
Bless all the dear children in thy tender care.
And take us to heaven to live with thee there.

O Little Town of Bethlehem

1. O lit - tle town of Beth - le - hem, How
2. O morn - ing stars, to - ge - - - ther Pro -

still we__ see thee lie! A - bove thy deep and
- claim the__ ho - ly Birth! And prai - ses sing to

dream - less__ sleep The si - lent stars go by. Yet
God__ the__ King, And peace to__ men on earth; For__

in thy dark__ streets__ shi - neth The
Christ is born__ of __ Ma - ry, And,

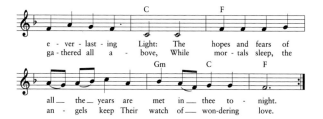

e - ver - last - ing Light: The hopes and fears of
ga - thered all a - bove, While mor - tals sleep, the

all __ the __ years are met in __ thee to - night.
an - gels keep Their watch of __ won-dering love.

How silently, how silently
The wondrous gift is given!
So God imparts to human hearts
The blessings of his heaven.
No ear may hear his coming,
But, in this world of sin,
Where meek souls will receive him, still
The dear Christ enters in.

Where children pure and happy
Pray to the blessed Child;
Where misery cries out to thee.
Son of the mother mild;
Where Charity stands watching
And Faith holds wide the door,
The dark night wakes, the glory breaks,
And Christmas comes once more.

O holy child of Bethlehem.
Descend to us we pray;
Cast out our sin, and enter in:
Be born in us today!
We hear the Christmas angels
The great glad tidings tell;
O come to us, abide with us.
Our Lord Emmanuel!

It Came Upon the Midnight Clear

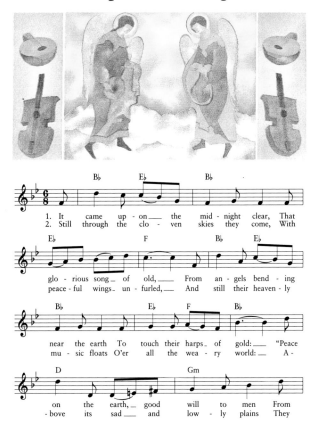

1. It came up-on__ the mid-night clear, That
2. Still through the clo-ven skies they come, With

glo - rious song__ of old,__ From an-gels bend - ing
peace-ful wings__ un-furled,__ And still their heaven-ly

near the earth To touch their harps__ of gold:__ "Peace
mu - sic floats O'er all the wea - ry world:__ A -

on the earth,__ good will to men From
- bove its sad__ and low - ly plains They

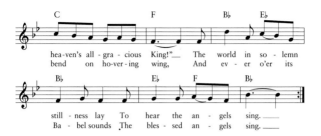

heav-en's all - gra - cious King!"__ The world in so - lemn
bend on ho-ver - ing wing, And ev - er o'er its

still - ness lay To hear the an - gels sing. _____
Ba - bel sounds The bles - sed an - gels sing. _____

Yet with the woes of sin and strife
The world has suffered long:
Beneath the angels' strain have rolled
Two thousand years of wrong,
And man, at war with man, hears not
The love-song which they bring:
O hush the noise, ye men of strife,
And hear the angels sing!

And ye, beneath life's crushing load,
Whose forms are bending low,
Who toil along the climbing way
With painful steps and slow,
Look now! for glad and golden hours
Come swiftly on the wing;
O rest beside the weary road,
And hear the angels sing!

For lo! the days are hastening on,
By prophet-bards foretold,
When, with the ever-circling years,
Come round the Age of Gold,
When peace shall over all the earth
Its ancient splendours fling,
And the whole world give back the song
Which now the angels sing.   ⁂

God Rest You Merry, Gentlemen

Em
God rest you merry, gen - tle - men, Let

B7   Em
no - thing you dis - may, Re - mem - ber Christ our

B7
Sa - viour was born on Christ - mas Day, To

Am   G   B7
save poor souls from Sa - tan's power That had

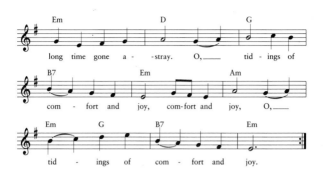

long time gone a- -stray. O,___ tid-ings of com-fort and joy, com-fort and joy, O,___ tid- ings of com - fort and joy.

From God that is our Father,
The blessed angels came,
Unto some certain shepherds,
With tidings of the same;
That there was born in Bethlehem,
The Son of God by name.

Chorus

Go, fear not, said God's angels,
Let nothing you affright,
For there is born in Bethlehem,
Of a pure Virgin bright,
One able to advance you,
And throw down Satan quite.

Chorus

The shepherds at those tidings,
Rejoiced much in mind,
And left their flocks a-feeding
In tempest storms of wind,
And straight they came to Bethlehem.
The Son of God to find.

Chorus

Now when they came to Bethlehem,
Where our sweet Saviour lay,
They found Him in a manger,
Where oxen feed on hay,
The blessed Virgin kneeling down,
Unto the Lord did pray.

Chorus

With sudden joy and gladness,
The shepherds were beguil'd,
To see the Babe of Israel,
Before his mother mild,
On them with joy and cheerfulness,
Rejoice each mother's child.

Chorus

Now to the Lord sing praises,
All you within this place,
Like we true loving brethren,
Each other to embrace,
For the merry time of Christmas,
Is drawing on apace.

Chorus

God bless the ruler of this house,
And send him long to reign,
And many a merry Christmas
May live to see again.
Among your friends and kindred,
That live both far and near,
And God send you a happy New Year.

Chorus

The First Nowell

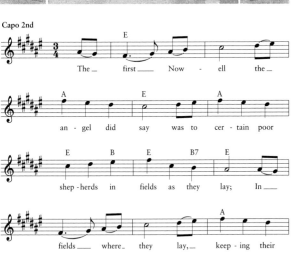

Capo 2nd

The _ first ____ Now - ell the _

an - gel did say was to cer - tain poor

shep -herds in fields as they lay; In ____

fields ____ where_ they lay,____ keep -ing their

sheep In a cold win-ter's night __ that was __ so deep; Now - ell, __ No - well, No - well, No - well, No - well! Born is the King __ of Is - ra - el!

They looked up and saw a star,
Shining in the east, beyond them far;
And to the earth it gave great light,
And so it continued both day and night:

Chorus

And by the light of that same star,
Three Wise Men came from country far;
To seek for a King was their intent,
And to follow the star wheresoever it went:

Chorus

This star drew nigh to the north-west;
O'er Bethlehem it took its rest,
And there it did both stop and stay
Right over the place where Jesus lay:

Chorus

Then did they know assuredly
Within that house the King did lie:
One entered in then for to see,
And found the Babe in poverty:

Chorus

Then entered in those Wise Men three,
Fell reverently upon their knee,
And offered there in His presence
Both gold and myrrh and frankincense:

Chorus

Between an ox-stall and an ass
This Child truly there born He was;
For want of clothing they did Him lay
All in the manger, among the hay:

Chorus

Then let us all with one accord
Sing praises to our heavenly Lord,
That hath made heaven and earth of naught,
And with His blood mankind hath bought:

Chorus

If we in our time shall do well,
We shall be free from death and hell;
For God hath prepared for us all
A resting place in general:

Chorus

Good King Wenceslas

1. Good King Wen - ces - las look'd out,
2. "Hi - ther, page, and stand by me,

On the Feast of Ste - phen, When the snow lay
If thou know - 'st, tel - ling, Yon - der pea - sant,

round a - bout, Deep and crisp and e - ven:
who is he? Where and what his dwel - ling?"

Bright - ly shone the moon that night, Though the frost was
"Sire, he lives a good league hence, Un - der - neath the

cru - el,   When a poor man   came in sight,
moun - tain,   Right a - gainst the   for - est fence,

gath -'ring win - ter fu - - el.
By Saint A - gnes' foun - - tain."

"Bring me flesh, and bring me wine,
Bring me pine logs hither:
Thou and I will see him dine,
When we bear them thither."
Page and monarch, forth they went,
Forth they went together;
Through the rude wind's wild lament
And the bitter weather.

"Sire, the night is darker now,
And the wind blows stronger;
Fails my heart, I know not how;
I can go no longer."
"Mark my footsteps, good my page;
Tread thou in them boldly:
Thou shalt find the winter's rage
Freeze thy blood less coldly."

In his master's steps he trod,
Where the snow lay dinted;
Heat was in the very sod
Which the Saint had printed.
Therefore, Christian men, be sure,
Wealth or rank possessing,
Ye who now will bless the poor,
Shall yourselves find blessing.

We Wish You a Merry Christmas

We wish you a merry Christ-mas, We wish you a merry Christ-mas, We wish you a mer-ry Christ-mas, And a Hap-py New Year! *Chorus:* Good tid-ings we bring To you and your kin, We

wish you a mer-ry Christ-mas And a hap-py New Year!

Now bring us some figgy pudding,
Now bring us some figgy pudding,
Now bring us some figgy pudding,
Now bring some to us here.

Chorus

We won't go until we get it,
We won't go until we get it,
We won't go until we get it,
So bring some right here.

Chorus

We all like our figgy pudding,
We all like our figgy pudding,
So bring us some figgy pudding,
With all its good cheer!

Chorus

Rocking

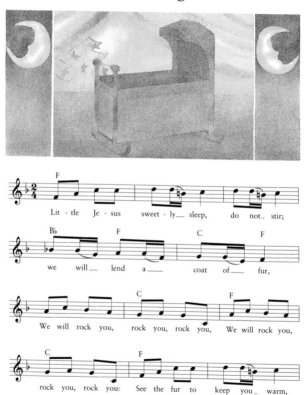

Lit - tle Je - sus sweet - ly sleep, do not stir;

we will lend a coat of fur,

We will rock you, rock you, rock you, We will rock you,

rock you, rock you: See the fur to keep you warm,

Snug - ly — round your — ti - ny — form.

Mary's little baby, sleep, sweetly sleep,
Sleep in comfort, slumber deep;
We will rock you, rock you, rock you,
We will rock you, rock you, rock you,
We will serve you all we can,
Darling, darling little man.

The Holly and the Ivy

The hol-ly and the i-vy, When they are both full grown, Of__ all the trees that are in the wood, The__ hol-ly bears the crown. The ris-ing of the sun __ And the run-ning of the deer, The __ play-ing of the

mer - ry or - gan, Sweet sing - ing in the choir.

The holly bears bears a blossom,
As white as the lily flower,
And Mary bore sweet Jesus Christ,
To be our sweet Saviour:

Chorus

The holly bears a berry,
As red as any blood,
And Mary bore sweet Jesus Christ
To do poor sinners good:

Chorus

The holly bears a prickle,
As sharp as any thorn,
And Mary bore sweet Jesus Christ
On Christmas day in the morn:

Chorus

The holly bears a bark,
As bitter as any gall,
And Mary bore sweet Jesus Christ
For to redeem us all:

Chorus

The holly and the ivy,
When they are both full grown,
Of all the trees that are in the wood,
The holly bears the crown.

Chorus

Wassail, Wassail, all over the Town

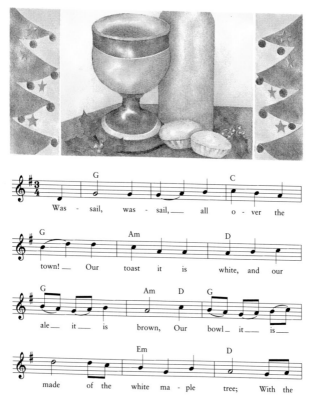

Was - sail, was - sail, ___ all o - ver the town! ___ Our toast it is white, and our ale __ it __ is brown, Our bowl _ it __ is __ made of the white ma - ple tree; With the

was - sail-ing bowl we'll drink — to thee.

So here is to Cherry and to his right cheek,
Pray God send our master a good piece of beef,
And a good piece of beef that may we all see;
With the wassailing bowl we'll drink to thee.

And here is to Dobbin and to his right eye,
Pray God send our master a good Christmas pie,
And a good Christmas pie that may we all see;
With our wassailing bowl we'll drink to thee.

So here is to Broad May and to her broad horn,
May God send our master a good crop of corn,
And a good crop of corn that may we all see;
With the wassailing bowl we'll drink to thee.

And here is to Fillpail and to her left ear;
Pray God send our master a happy New Year,
And a happy New Year as e'er he did see;
With our wassailing bowl we'll drink to thee.

And here is to Colly and to her left tail,
Pray God send our master he never may fail
A bowl of strong beer; I pray you draw near,
And our jolly wassail it's then you shall hear.

Come, butler, come fill us a bowl of the best,
Then we hope that your soul in heaven may rest;
But if you do draw us a bowl of the small,
Then down shall do butler, bowl and all.

Then here's to the maid in the lily white smock,
Who tripped to the door and slipped back the lock!
Who tripped to the door and pulled back the pin,
For to let these jolly wassailers in.

Once, in Royal David's City

Once, in roy-al Da-vid's ci-ty, Stood a low-ly cat-tle shed Where a mo-ther laid her ba-by In a man-ger for his bed; Ma-ry was that mo-ther mild, Je-sus Christ her on-ly child.

beau - ty bright, West - ward lead - ing, still pro - ceed - ing, Guide us to thy per - fect light.

Born a king on Bethlehem plain,
Gold I bring to crown him again,
King for ever, ceasing never
Over us all to reign.

Chorus

Frankincense to offer have I,
Incense owns a Deity nigh;
Prayer and praising all men raising,
Worship him, God on high.

Chorus

Myrrh is mine; its bitter perfume
Breathes a life of gathering gloom;
Sorrowing, sighing, bleeding, dying,
Sealed in the stone-cold tomb.

Chorus

Glorious now behold him arise,
King, and God, and sacrifice.
Heaven sing:'Alleluia';
'Alleluia' the earth replies.

Chorus

See, Amid the Winter's Snow

See, a-mid the win-ter's snow, Born for us on
earth be-low, See the ten-der Lamb ap-pears,
Pro-mised from e-ter-nal years! *Chorus:* Hail, thou e-ver-
-bless-ed morn! Hail, Re-demp-tion's hap-py dawn!

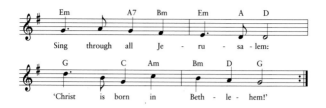

Sing through all Je - ru - sa - lem:

'Christ is born in Beth - le - hem!'

Lo! within a manger lies
He who built the starry skies,
He who, throned in height sublime,
Sits the Cherubim.

Chorus

Say, ye holy shepherds, say:
What's your joyful news today?
Wherefore have ye left your sheep
On the lonely mountain steep?

Chorus

'As we watched at dead of night,
Lo! we saw a wondrous light;
Angels, singing "Peace on earth",
Told us of the Saviour's birth.'

Chorus

Sacred Infant, all-divine,
What a tender was thine
Thus to come from highest bliss
Down to such a world as this!

Chorus

Teach, oh teach us, holy Child,
By thy face so meek and mild,
Teach us to resemble thee
In thy sweet humlity!

Chorus

Angels We Have Heard On High

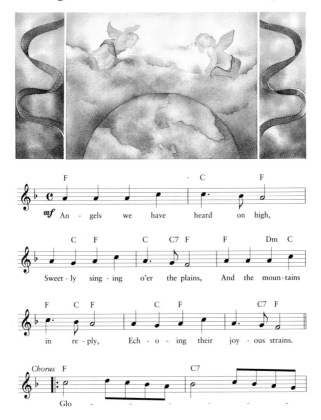

mf An - gels we have heard on high,

Sweet - ly sing - ing o'er the plains, And the moun - tains

in re - ply, Ech - o - ing their joy - ous strains.

Chorus Glo -

- - - ri - a *f* in ex - cel - sis

De - o, De - o.

Shepherds, why this jubilee?
Why your joyous strains prolong?
What the gladsome tidings be
Which inspire your heav'ly song?

Chorus

Come to Bethlehem and see
Him Whose birth the angels sing;
Come, adore on bended knee,
Christ the Lord, the newborn King.

Chorus

See Him in a manger laid,
Whom the choirs of angels praise;
Mary, Joseph, lend your aid,
While our hearts in love we raise.

Chorus

Joy to the World

Joy to the world, the Lord is come!

Let earth re-ceive her King; Let

eve-ry heart pre-pare him room,

and heav'n and na-ture sing, And heav'n and na-ture sing, And

heav'n,— and heav'n ____ and na - ture sing.

Joy to the world! the Saviour reigns;
Let men their songs employ,
While fields and floods, rocks, hills and plains
Repeat the sounding joy, repeat the sounding joy,
Repeat, repeat the sounding joy.

He rules the world with truth and grace,
And makes the nations prove
The glories of his righteousness
And wonders of his love, and wonders of his love,
And wonders, wonders of his love.

What Child is This

shep - herds guard and an - gels sing: Haste, haste _ to bring him laud, The Babe, _ the Son _ of Ma - ry!

Why lies he in such mean estate
Where ox and ass are feeding?
Good Christians fear: for sinners here
The silent Word is pleading.
Nail, spear shall pierce him through,
The Cross be borne for me, for you;
Hail! hail the Word Made Flesh,
The Babe, the Son of Mercy!

So bring him incense, gold and myrrh:
Come, peasant, king, to own him!
The Kings of Kings salvation brings:
Let loving hearts enthrone him!
Raising the song on high!
The Virgin sings her lullaby.
Joy, joy for Christ is born,
The Babe, the Son of Mary!

O Christmas Tree

mf O Christ-mas tree, O Christ-mas tree, How

green are thy branch-es; Thou stand-est in the

for - est wide In sum - mer-time, in

win -ter -tide, O Christ- mas tree, O

Christ-mas tree, How green are thy branch-es

O Christmas tree, O Christmas tree
Thy lights they shine so merry;
And every light it is a star
That shineth near and shineth far,
O Christmas tree, O Christmas tree
Thy lights they shine so merry.

O Christmas tree, O Christmas tree
Defying wind and weather;
Standing a-glitter through the night,
While snowflakes fall so soft and light,
O Christmas tree, O Christmas tree
Defying wind and weather.

O Christmas tree, O Christmas tree
Thou art so strong and steady;
When gladsome Yule doth come along
Though sing'st to God thy Christmas song,
O Christmas tree, O Christmas tree
Thou art so strong and steady.

The Twelve Days of Christmas

1. On the first day of Christ-mas my true love sent to me a par-tridge in a pear tree.

2. On the se-cond day of Christ-mas my true love sent to me two tur-tle doves, and a

par - tridge in a pear tree. 3. On the

third day of Christ-mas my true love sent to me

three French hens, 4. On the fourth day of Christ - mas my

true love sent to me four cal - ly birds, 5. On the

fifth day of Christ-mas my true love sent to me five gold

rings, four cal - ly birds, three French hens,

two__ tur - tle doves, and a par - tridge in a pear

tree. 6. On the sixth day of Christ - mas my
7. On the seventh
8. On the eighth
9. On the ninth
10. On the tenth
11. On the eleventh
12. On the twelfth

true love sent to me six geese a - lay - ing,
seven swans a - swim - ming,
eight maids a - milk - ing,
nine la - dies dan - cing,
ten lords a - leap - ing,
eleven pi - pers pi - ping,
twelve drum - mers drum - ming,